THE TAO OF
MOTHERHOOD

VIMALA McCLURE

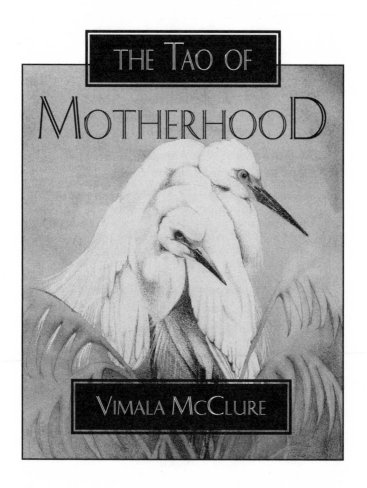

THE TAO OF
MOTHERHOOD

VIMALA MCCLURE

NEW WORLD LIBRARY
NOVATO, CALIFORNIA

New World Library
14 Pamaron Way
Novato, California 94949

Cover and text design by Linda Corwin
Cover/interior illustrations by Susan Pinkerton

Library of Congress Cataloging-in-Publication Data

McClure, Vimala Schneider, 1952-
The Tao of motherhood / Vimala McClure.
    p.   cm.
Adaptation of: Tao te ching.
Originally published: Willow Springs, Mo. :
Nucleus Publications, 1991.
Includes bibliographical references.
ISBN 1-57731-014-4 (pbk. : alk. paper)
1. Parenting — Religious aspects — Taoism.
2. Lao-tzu. Tao te ching
I. Lao-tzu. Tao te ching
II. Title.

BL 1923.M38 1997   96-47177
649'. 1—dc21   CIP

First printing, April 1997
Printed in Canada on acid-free paper
ISBN 1-57731-014-4
Distributed to the trade by Publishers Group West
10 9 8 7

Dedicated to my mother

CONTENTS

FOREWORD

Motherhood is both heart-lifting and heart-wrenching. What lifts our hearts more than the sweet experience of having a sleepy baby snuggle cozily into our necks, contentedly making those magical baby sounds? What causes our hearts to soar higher than receiving a spontaneous "I love you, Mom!" accompanied by an enthusiastic hug? What fills us with more quiet joy than watching our children grow into self-confident, happy, and loving adults? For me, family and motherhood have brought the most profound joy and fulfillment of my life.

Paradoxically, along with the joys come the sorrows. And, while my life has been filled to the brim with both bliss and sadness, nothing has caused more excruciating pain than watching my children suffer through illness and trauma, or fearing for their safety, or going through periods of emotional distance from them. Elizabeth Stone described the depth of feeling involved in mothering beautifully when she said, "Making the decision to have a child — it's wondrous. It is to decide forever to have your heart go walking around outside your body." How I wish that I'd had *The Tao of Motherhood* as a comfort and guide when my four "outside hearts" were little. How thankful I am to have discovered it even now when they are adults! Reading it has helped honor my motherhood and mothering — both the strengths and weaknesses — and helped me relax into the flow of the new adventure of grandparenting. The wisdom of the teachings still apply, for, as we all know, once a mother, forever a mother.

Over the years, I've come to believe that the act of parenting is a cleansing tempest in which our souls are given myriad opportunities to gain new strength, wisdom, and serenity. *The Tao of Motherhood* is a discerning guide, a comforting companion, and a soul friend for those of us navigating the mysterious waters of motherhood. In savoring this book, let it teach you to trust your intuition and to be gentle with yourself as you mother both your own inner child and the children given to your care. I know in my heart that you will find treasures for your soul in Vimala's shared wisdom and in the inspiration of the remarkable Taoist teacher, Lao Tzu.

— Sue Patton Thoele

Sue Patton Thoele is the author of Heart Centered Marriage, The Courage To Be Yourself, The Woman's Book of Courage, The Woman's Book of Confidence, The Woman's Book of Spirit, *and* Autumn of the Spring Chicken.

Twenty years ago, on a summer's evening, I slipped into a chair on a big porch in Denver, Colorado and listened to Vimala sing. I sat behind her, hoping that my presence would not disturb the sweet music and devotional sentiment that brought tears to my eyes. Today as I read *The Tao of Motherhood* new tears came, and reminded me of those tears years ago.

During the first years I knew Vimala in Denver, we both worked in a large house filled with young people trying to guide a spiritual and social service organization. I remember Vimala as a quiet but powerful soul who seemed to stay out of the battles, but always got what she needed. Someone who sat back and watched what went on and then made the precise move needed to reestablish balance.

When Vimala does take action, she pours herself into it, leaving a clear path behind her for those who might follow. When she had to give birth by

Caesarean section and felt unprepared for the experience, she helped form the Caesarean Birth Education
Group in Boulder, Colorado in 1977. After seeing
infant massage when she worked in an orphanage in
India, she tried it out, very successfully, with her col-
icky son. She began teaching other parents, and by
the time her second baby was born, she was teaching
others to be instructors. From those small beginnings
has grown The International Association of Infant
Massage Instructors, which now has instructors
teaching parents to massage their babies in fifteen
countries.

When Vimala sees a need, she looks for practical
ways that she can make a difference. While others
may talk or complain, Vimala takes action. When her
spiritual teacher was being mistreated in prison, she
compiled the evidence and wrote a book to spread the
information. She wanted to learn Bengali, so she put
together a super learning program to help others, and
became a proficient speaker in the process. When she

fell in love with Bangladesh, she wrote a book for children, called *Bangladesh: Rivers in a Crowded Land*. To help women apply spirituality to their lives, she produced *A Woman's Guide to Tantra Yoga*.

The Tao of Motherhood has grown out of a period in Vimala's life when she has seen her children grow both closer to her and further away. She has watched them become teenagers, struggle with family changes, and make decisions that stretched her as their mother. She has formed a new family from two, watching the years it took for balance to again settle in.

As with all true artists, both pain and joy have contributed to her work. Vimala has struggled with poverty, health problems, and abuse at different times in her life. But she has taken them and mixed them with deep thought, love, and spiritual bliss, and come up with the inspiration and discipline to manifest practical works. Works such as *The Tao of Motherhood*, which, though based on an ancient text, helps us parent in a very modern, very stressful world.

One last story to share. I attended a training of infant massage instructors that Vimala was leading in 1984. One father in the demonstration class was particularly rough with his baby, just simply because he was a big and tough, but loving, person. When a concerned trainee asked if we shouldn't be trying to temper his enthusiasm in order to protect the baby, Vimala pointed out, "Remember that every child and every parent has a completely unique and special relationship. That child knows his dad and loves his dad. Our job is to watch that communication, to nurture it, and to support the parents in their heart-to-heart relationships with their children." I see that idea, too, in *The Tao of Motherhood*.

You and your child have a unique and very special relationship. The dos and don'ts of all the advice givers out there may or may not apply to you. You have to listen to your heart and to your child and then make the decisions that are good for right now, for you two.

A lot of water has flowed under the bridge in the twenty years I have known Vimala. I now have four children, and she has three. Like other mothers and women everywhere throughout time, we reach out to each other to share our joys and fears, our spirituality, our reality and yes, our tears.

May your parenting be fulfilling and satisfying for both you and your little ones.

— Jody Wright

Jody Wright is the mother of four daughters, a founding member of the International Association of Infant Massage Instructors, a La Leche League Leader, and with her husband, Prakash Laufer, the owner of Motherwear, a catalog designed for nursing mothers.

═══ INTRODUCTION ═══

Since before the birth of my first child, parenting has been an important and integral part of my spiritual path. Having meditated daily for several years before my first pregnancy, I wanted to continue my practice. But I knew that pregnancy and young children added a level of chaos into life which seemed to be in conflict with the stillness and quiet — the solitude — of meditation. My search for a way to continue functioning as a spiritual seeker led to much thinking about spirituality and its place in everyday life.

When my first child was born it was time for me to begin practicing in earnest a lesson which was part of my instruction in meditation. The lesson is called *madhuvidya* in Sanskrit ("sweet knowledge"), and it is the act of infusing spirituality into every aspect of life. It is the conscious process of perceiving the unity of all things, of trying to understand deep within oneself that everything is sacred. Infant massage was a wonderful tool, and became an important part of my relationship with my children. I shared this with other parents in my book *Infant Massage: A Handbook for Loving Parents.*

As my children grew our relationships provided so much growth for me. In order to give them what they needed — respect, acceptance, encouragement, boundaries, assistance, understanding, and above all unconditional love — I had to learn about these things for myself. Everything I had learned about spirituality was tested. Children are mirrors; they will always show you exactly what is going on inside of you. Each phase of their growth is an opportunity to heal your own pain, to go deeper inside yourself and become more truly human.

Parenting is a spiritual path that can bring you great pain and great joy and that can have a tremendous positive impact on your personality and behavior. I believe our children, unknowingly and with innocent trickery, teach us the deeper knowledge of how to be a true human being.

My heart has learned its lessons from meditation and mothering. This book has given me a chance to distill some of those lessons through the vehicle of the wonderful Taoist teachings of Lao Tzu.

I hope you find inspiration here, and that your journey with your child is a joyful one that teaches you what you came here to learn.

— Vimala McClure

ONENESS

Tao is the oneness of all things.

You and your child come from
One and journey toward One.
You are essentially the same.

Right mothering springs from
this knowledge: the One in either
responds to the One in both.
The bond is oneness, and cannot
be broken.

When doubt and uncertainty
arise, return to this simple truth.

Be in oneness and the illusion of separateness dies.

Be still and allow unity to be revealed.

DETACHMENT

Like the eternal Tao, a wise mother gives birth but does not possess. She meets the child's needs yet requires no gratitude.

Observe how great masters raise up their dearest disciples. Observe how nature raises up the plants and animals.

Great teachers take no credit for their students' growth, yet they will go to any length to teach them what they need to know.

Nature requires no praise,
yet it provides for the needs
of earth's inhabitants.

Mother is the reflective principle,
the balancing agent for the child.
Like a guru, she allows the child to
make mistakes and loves the child
without condition. Like nature,
she allows consequences to unfold
and balance to be restored when
it is lost.

She intervenes only when the
right use of power is required.

3

RESPONSE

Right mothering meets the
child's need.

Focusing on what the child should
not be draws resistant energy.
Pointing out what the child *should*
be feeds self-hatred and struggle.

Ask yourself, "What is my child
telling me about his needs at this
moment?" This is not always easy.
One child's needs may be more
obvious — or more acceptable —
than another's.

Meeting needs and obeying
commands are not the same.
The wise obey the Divine Law
and thus fulfill the need of the
moment through action or
non-action. They are responsive,
not tyrannized.

This has nothing to do with what
society says is proper. It has
everything to do with the Infinite
Good as it flows through the
here and now.

Do not reward performance.
Rather, respond to Spirit
expressing the Way. You are a
mirror with which your child
sees — and corrects — himself.

4

PERSPECTIVE

Remember, you and your child are travelers through infinite time. How you interact is important enough to change lifetimes of karma; yet it is an insignificant drop in the ocean of relationship through which you both move.

Keep in mind the endless nature of being, and your journey will gain perspective.

5

RESPECT

Raise up your children with great reverence for the Consciousness that moves in them. Treat them with respect, even in their infancy, for they are not yours.

Reverence and respect are not the same as worship; children thrive on benevolent neglect.

The child who feels your respect during silences is nourished more than the child who is constantly fussed and chattered over.

6

FEMININE

Mother is the feminine principle.
She represents the yin, the anima,
the receptive, the earth.
Though she must at times take
the role of the masculine principle,
it is the feminine which gives
her power and from which
she draws her strength.

She teaches her daughters to
respect their feminine nature.
She teaches her sons to respect
their feminine side and thus
all women.

The truly feminine mother
never cringes or defers.
Her strength is unshakable,
like the earth upon which we
walk but which can topple us
with a single deep breath.

7

SELFLESSNESS

Everything which endures can
only do so because Eternal
Consciousness gives it sentience.

A mother who gives herself
completely to her infant meets
herself in the dark and finds
fulfillment.

In the hours between midnight
and dawn, she crosses the
threshold of self-concern and
discovers a Self that has no limits.
A wise mother meets this
Presence with humility and steps
through time into selflessness.

Infants know when their mothers
have done this, and they
become peaceful.

Who, then, is the doer? Is it the
infant who brings its mother
through the veil of self-concern
into limitlessness? Is it the
mother, who chooses to hold
sacred her infant's needs and
surrender herself? Or is it the
One, which weaves them both
through a spiraling path
toward wholeness?

You can sit and meditate while
your baby cries himself to sleep.
Or you can go to him and share
his tears, and find your Self.

8

ACCEPTANCE

Water benefits us without taking
from us. It cleanses us, nourishes
us, and calms our restlessness.

So is a mother to her child. From
the moment of birth, a child's
well-being is her only concern.

A wise mother cleans and discards
the child's waste without com-
ment. The child's excrement, its
tears, its rages, are all allowed to
be and discarded without emotion.

A wise mother does not judge
her child.

9

POWER

There is great power in being a
mother. It is easy to think you
control your child and his destiny;
that you can mold him into
your ideal; that his imperfections
are yours to correct.

The power of a mother's love
is like gold in a temple.
Used for personal aggrandizement
it brings pain and suffering.
Hoarded, it benefits no one.
Used rightly, with benevolence,
in time of great need, it serves.

When you are about to use
your power in your relationship
with your child, think again.
Is there another way to
accomplish your goal?

Retreat and be still. Contemplate
your choices. When you choose to
use your power, use it justly, with
great calm, and do not waiver.

CLARITY

Strive for clarity in your own life.
What motivates your feelings?
We often live out the past over
and over in our relationships.
We sometimes fail to see
the real child, for we have
superimposed our own pain
upon our children.

Clear yourself. Find the child
within you, heal her, and set her
free. As long as the child in you
weeps and cringes, your power
as a mother will remain confused.

Polish the mirror of the self
and your child will see herself
more clearly.

11

EMPTY SPACES

The empty spaces make
wholeness. The emptiness in a
pot makes it valuable; you can
fill it with food or water.

Pay attention to what isn't. Listen
for what your child does not say.
Observe what she does not do.

Similarly, know that your child
uses your empty spaces. What
you do not say resounds. What
you do not do impresses.

12

PEACE

Life with children is naturally
noisy. Can you find the silence
within the noise? Can you feel
the peace within the turmoil?

If you cannot reflect in the chaos
of the moment, withdraw.
Make time for yourself to turn
inward and digest your life.

Whether you realize it or not,
Mother is the pivot of the family.
Not you, but the eternal Mother
expressing Itself through
your choices.

To allow the Mother principle to
work to center your family,
take time for yourself. Otherwise,
the self will be constantly
grasping for its share. This
grasping obscures the Mother
principle from within you and
from your family, and leaves
everyone alone and lost.

13

SELF-CARE

It is said, "She who values her body more than dominion over the empire can be given custody of the empire." Taking care of yourself is your right and your responsibility.

If a mother values herself, her children value her. She teaches self-esteem by her example. Her peaceful demeanor communicates love to all who come in contact with her.

Knowing when to sacrifice the self
and when to nurture the self
comes with daily mindfulness.
Pay attention to your body's
signals. Observing your feelings
each day, eventually you will be
able to take time for yourself
before it becomes an angry
demand. This enables you to give
of yourself appropriately, without
resentment.

14

LOVE

Parenting is at times confusing. There will be moments when you truly do not know. Should you exert your authority or step back? Should you give advice or remain silent? Should you offer help or allow a mistake to be made?

When you cannot see what is happening, relax and look gently with your inner eye. The harder you try to take hold of a situation, the more difficult it becomes.

Let go. Trust in the Way which follows its own flow.

Allow the Great to live in you
and work through you
for your child's greater good.

Return to the core: a relationship
of love is more worthwhile than
a philosophical position. When
doubt arises, give way only
to love.

15

OUR FOREMOTHERS

The ancient teachers demonstrated
their realization of the Way.
These ancient teachers were often
women. They were mothers and
sisters, aunts, and grandmothers.
They meditated. Through their
relationships, they taught the
art of being.

Because they meditated, their
depth made them seem inscrutable
and their wisdom profound.
The truth is, they simply knew
how to be human.

They observed behaviors and acted with precision and care, never acting recklessly. They behaved with dignity and grace and won the respect of others without trying. They respected others and treated children as human beings.

They were strong yet yielding, like ice ready to melt. They were simple, like the uncarved block of wood. They were receptive like a valley between high mountains.

They were full of life and involved in their families, yet they were able to be still and become as deep and clear as pure water.

These ancient grandmothers did not need to go away into the caves or forests to become enlightened. They were enlightenment itself.

16

AWARENESS

Everything arises from
Consciousness and returns.

The universe is the play of the
rising and returning of millions
of beings, all becoming One.
You and your child are both on
this path too.

It is impossible to keep this
awareness of your destiny
awakened all the time. But daily
meditation can bring awareness
to your thoughts and actions.

Awareness brings constancy to your relationships. Constancy allows your child to release fear and follow his destiny.

Meditate on Oneness. Release the small self to the Infinite, and the Infinite will take care of Itself.

17

TRUST

A wise mother does not unnecessarily interfere with her child's life.

Your children have their own process — their own thoughts, feelings, and reactions — which must be allowed to unfold.

If your childhood was painful you may get overinvolved with your children's lives and smother them. Or you may find yourself forcing them to think and feel the way you do, to adopt all your values and live the life you wish you had.

If you do not trust your children's process, your children cannot trust anyone or anything. Your confidence in them builds their confidence in themselves.

Assist your children in such a way that they think, "We did it ourselves!"

18

HYPOCRISY

When you forget that you and your children are instruments of the One, dogma takes over.

You begin to think in judgments of yourself and others:

"All mothers should *(stay home, have a career, be involved with school, help with homework, keep a spotless home...)*, therefore I'm not a good mother if I don't."

Or, "All children should *(be polite, respect their elders, help at home,*

*get good grades, win in sports, be
popular, appreciate good music,
read great books...),* therefore my
children are bad if they don't."

When truth is forgotten,
acceptance, tolerance, compassion,
and flexibility give way to
judgment, intolerance,
meanness, and rigidity.
Hypocrisy follows.

Children who are closer to their
birth and thus to the experience of
Oneness, rightly reject hypocrisy.

19

RETURN

Throw away gadgets. Discard
expert opinions. Forget the toys
to stimulate intelligence. Don't
buy devices to simulate what is
real.

Return to the real. Connect with
your children heart to heart.
Let them gaze at you, at trees
and water and sky. Let them feel
their pain. Feel it with them.

Touch them with your hands,
your eyes, and your heart.
Let them bond with the living,
breathing world. Let them feel
their feelings and teach them
their names.

Return to the uncarved simplicity.

20

EDUCATION

The real education teaches us to
be whole human beings.

Be concerned with this: that you,
your marriage, and your home
teach health and balance
and truth.

Any further education merely
augments this basic course.

21

SPIRITUALITY

The wise remain aware of the spirituality of life.

Every mother has felt the stillness and the stir of Eternal Consciousness in her womb. Remember that.

Bring that mysterious, silent moment into the clamoring present.

SURRENDER

Truth is in paradox:

Surrender and you get
everything. Bend and be strong.

When you reach your limit and
are exhausted, new energy rises
in you. When you release
others, they come to you.
The wise know this: Let go
in order to preserve.

Be empty and fulfilled.

STOP

There is no natural pouring-forth that lasts forever. When it rains, it stops. The wind blows, and then it ceases.

Learn to use your words wisely, to communicate rather than to lecture. Speak your truth, state your feelings, then stop. Your actions, in silence, speak louder and will be heard.

Teach your children this:
A human being is greater than
a human doing.

SECURITY

Your children are not you.

To try to show the world what a
good mother you are diminishes
you. To try to show the world
what good children you have
diminishes them.

Heal your insecurity by holding
to the truth. The One Consciousness flows through all without
boasting.

Dependence

Eternal Consciousness is not
a thing. It has many names and
no name. It is within and beyond
everything. It is the essence of
us all.

Your child depends on you. You
depend on the earth. The earth
depends on the universe. The
universe depends on the Supreme.

The Supreme is subject to
nothing. It is the Great Mother,
and She holds you in the palm
of her hand.

26

CENTER

Pay attention and stay centered.

You carry the mantle of "Mother,"
the eternal principle of balance and
stability.

When your children's energy is
scattered, be grounded. When
your children throw tantrums,
be still. Know what you stand for.

Be firm and consistent to teach your
children about boundaries. Thus you
will root them in health and release
their souls to limitlessness.

KNOWLEDGE

Someone who travels often knows the best routes. Someone who speaks for a living knows when to pause. Someone who works with numbers knows how to add and subtract in her head.

A wise mother knows: It is her state of consciousness that matters.

Her gentleness and clarity command respect. Her love creates security.

To learn the Way, children need
to respect the Mother. To learn the
Way, mothers need to cherish the
Child.

Thus each follows nature and
finds the Self.

HEALING

A mother must know how to
assert her warrior side, how to
wield power and make decisions,
how to inspire discipline and set
boundaries. But she must hold to
the feminine to be truly effective.

The most powerful mothers are
healers. Their surgeon's knives
cut but do not sever. They nourish
and listen.

A wise mother knows the One
Consciousness works through her.

INTERVENTION

Avoid pushing too hard. Your
children are full of spirit and
will find their way. Their true
parent resides within them;
you are only a reflection.

Mothers who constantly interfere
— who push and challenge,
who lecture and berate —
think they are molding their
children into good citizens.
In fact, they are destroying
confidence and inviting scorn.

Know when to intervene and how.
Do it with gentleness, firmness,
swiftness, and respect. And then
release the child to the Way.

30

CONFLICT

Your children will challenge you
and your power. Do not use force
or intimidation to manage them.

Remember, wars bring suffering
to all. The winners and the losers
both have bitter harvests.

When your child engages you in
conflict, bring it full circle without
physical, mental, or emotional
violence.

Withdraw, be still. Try to
understand what the child needs,
whether it be a firm boundary
or a listening heart. Then calmly
exert your authority with love,
end the conflict and restore
harmony.

31

ANGER

When you feel angry with your child, know that something rational must be done. State your feelings honestly, then withdraw to process your emotions and make a plan.

Striking out, either physically or emotionally, may succeed in getting through to the child, but it will also plant the seeds of guilt. Guilt is followed by resentment and bitterness. A victory can therefore end in failure.

Too many such victories and you will witness the death of your child's trust.

32

THE WAY

The Way cannot be defined;
it is only when you are in its flow
that it becomes known to you.

If parents, the guardians of the
human race, could hold to the
Way, children would naturally
grow strong and healthy in body,
mind, and spirit. Nothing special
would be needed.

Because we have forgotten
the Way, roadmaps and
instructions have come into being.

One must know when to put aside
the instructions and find the Way.

The single most important
instruction is this: Meditate on the
Eternal. As the river finds the sea,
you will find the Way.

CONTENTMENT

You can know your children with
some intelligence. Knowing
yourself requires enlightenment.

You can manage your children
with strength. Mastering your
own life requires true power.

To accept what you are is to be
content, and contentment is the
greatest wealth. To work with
patience is to gather power.
To surrender to the Eternal flow
is to be completely present.

THE ETERNAL SOURCE

Eternal Consciousness is
everywhere, in everything.
Everything depends on it and it
guides all things.

Though it is the source of every
atom of the universe, nothing can
affect it. No one can own it.
It lives in every blade of grass
and every human being, without
discrimination.

A wise mother is like the
Eternal One. She shines in her
children's eyes.

VALUES

If you hold to the Eternal
in thought, word, and action,
your children will return
again and again to you.

Your children may not
understand the depth of your
parenting until later. They may
question your values and say
you are "weird" or not like other
kids' parents.

They may say your life is boring
or strange. Never mind. The wise
are not caught up in appearances.

The Way is at times boring in
its simplicity. Hold to it. The
superficial eventually repels.

That which is real attracts every
good thing to it.

36

Upside-Down

If you want to know what to do,
learn to look at things upside-
down. To receive, you must give.
Those who boast are insecure.
Silence speaks louder than words.
The strongest warrior never
shows his sword. The soft
overcomes the hard.

Here is an exercise: When you
feel a hardness come around
your heart, go soft and explore
the sensations and feelings that
arise. Feel what is beneath anger:
thousands of tiny moments of

pain, confusion, doubt, fear,
self-protection. Accept all this
as part of you. Look on yourself
with kindness.

Now notice the quality of your
heart. How different it is from the
hard edge of control that springs
from fear.

DOING

A wise parent does little,
yet so much gets done!

After all, the Eternal does nothing,
yet the entire universe goes on.

When you get too busy, stop and
return to center. When you are
centered, you easily keep things
in order. When things are in order,
there is not much to do.

A wise parent does little,
yet so much gets done!

CHOICE

If you leave parenting to the
unconscious process, you will
blindly repeat unhealthy
parenting you may have received.

If your childhood was not happy
and secure, you may try too hard
to be an ideal parent.

There are choices to be made
every day. Reject the rigid
and favor the firm. Reject
criticism and favor support.
Reject permissiveness and favor
negotiation. Reject abandonment
and favor direction.

Choose the fruit, not the flower.
Choose the berry, not the chaff.
Choose the inner, not the outer.

Conscious choice is the hallmark
of healthy parenting.

39

NATURE

There is a natural order of things:
the seasons change, the tides well
up and recede, the moon circles
and women's bodies respond.

The sky is clear. The earth is solid.
The unseen forces are powerful.
The valley is full of life. Every
atom dances with Consciousness.

Look around: Everything follows
its nature; wholeness results.

Imagine what would happen if
nature did not follow its biological
programming.

The sky would shatter. The earth would explode. The unseen forces would run amok. The valley would go barren. Everything would lose Consciousness and die into the void.

Oneness is the root of balance. When you can follow your own nature in balance, you will provide exactly what your children need.

40

BEING

We all come from the One and return to it.

Stop and bring your consciousness into this moment. Let your heart absorb your mind. Can you feel the oneness that connects you with your child?

Surrendering to the One is the Way.

Everything comes from Being. Being springs from that which is beyond Being.

LISTENING

A wise mother learns each day
from quiet listening. Her
parenting springs from her
children's changing needs.

An average mother hears the
lessons but wonders how to be,
and forgets what she learns.
She is often filled with guilt and
is indecisive and irritable.

A foolish mother dismisses
what her soul hears in favor of
what the experts tell her.
She is rigid and controlling,
boastful and full of fear.

The best parenting springs from
simple love. The wise attune
themselves to a child's true need
and steadfastly follow it. Thus,
they cannot be called "permissive"
or "harsh."

What is right for each child
may not be right for all children.
What is right cannot always be
proven in a laboratory.

42

CYCLES

The One is born from beyond
One. One becomes two, and
two becomes three.

That which is beyond
consciousness gives birth to
consciousness, which gives birth
to mind, which gives birth
to matter and all the ten thousand
things. The ten thousand things
maintain a balance between
centrifugal and centripetal forces.

The ten thousand things hold
Eternal Consciousness within
them and thus are magnetized
back to the One.

Things harmonize opposites and
seek the One.

You must be a child to be a parent.
The infant is parent to its mother.

To move in balance toward One,
make sure you learn more from
your child than you teach her.

SOFTNESS

Soft overcomes hard.
Who you are means more to
your child than what you teach.

When your heart is hard
and the bitter taste of strong
words is in your mouth,
step back.

Let mind go into soft heart.
Breathe kindness and remain
quiet.

RELEASE

Which is dearer to you:
being right or being respected?

Being respected or being loved?

Having or being?

Know when to let your child go,
to have her own life and feelings.
Your security is within you,
not within your child.

Grasp and you will lose. Release
and find contentment.

SERENITY

The best mothering
looks like no mothering.

Smothering heats up, stillness
cools. Be a still, cool stream
for your child's agitation.

A serene mother rocks the
universe in her arms and
all is well.

WAR

When your life is in order,
your child finds balance.

When you cease to listen with
your heart, war breaks out.
When you lose sight of the big
picture, you fight and quarrel
over trifles and no one wins.

There is no greater pain
than feeling you are not enough.

Your child is enough, right now,
just the way he is. And so are you.

WHAT MATTERS

All you need to know
is within you.

Your child's spirit teaches
you how to guide her.

Be present. What is happening
right now? Be still and
comprehend with your inner
senses. Talk to the inner child,
setting aside theories.

If your child was taken from
you tomorrow, would this
matter today?

RELAX

First time mothers read all the books and cling to theories and gadgets.

Fifth time mothers have taken it all in and let it sink into the unconscious. Equipment has worn out and the child is given wooden spoons and the easy company of present-focused people.

The youngest child is usually the most relaxed!

49

THE PARTICULAR

Be open to your child's individual
needs and expression. One child
needs stimulation, the next needs
quiet. One needs to be carried all
the time, another likes to play
nearby with the freedom to
extend his limbs.

A wise mother knows: There is no
good child and no bad child.
There is only *this* child.

50

FEAR

When you have your first child,
suddenly life becomes precious.
So precious you can strangle it
with the tension of holding on.

What mother hasn't had fearful
fantasies of losing her child?
This is the hardest time to accept
letting go as part of holding on.

Three mothers in ten grasp their
children with claws of steel
to protect them from harm.

Three mothers in ten allow their
children to wander into danger.

Three mothers in ten confuse their
children with endless admonitions
and worries, yet force them
to face pain before they are ready.

Only ten percent accept the wheel
of life as it is. They are free from
fear, for they know that nothing
is ever lost. They do not grasp
and cling or organize their lives
around a fantasy of what might
happen.

For their children, fear cannot find
a place to lodge its blade.

51

FLOW

Everything comes from One
consciousness. The harmonious
rhythms we call happiness.
The discordant rhythms
we call pain.

Your child is attracted to the
One in you, to the Way which
nurtures, shelters, guides, and
protects. It flows from you, harmonious with the world from
which your child has come.

The Supreme nurtures without grasping, shelters without claiming, guides without interfering, and protects without smothering.

The closer you are to the Way, the more your child will trust you.

52

SIGNIFICANCE

The Mother of all is that from
which you draw your mothering.
It is the eternal balance, the
breathing, beating womb from
which all creation arises.
It is eternally giving birth,
eternally conceiving.

Close your mouth and allow the
Mother of all to speak in you.

Keep busy, fluttering and
chattering, and you cannot hear
Her voice.

Observe the child to know
the mother.

Observe the insignificant to know
what matters.

53

CONSUMPTION

A wise mother keeps her child's life simple. She gives away ten thousand toys and keeps only that which is useful.

She lets her baby gaze into her face and at the wondrous colors of nature.

She gives her child household things and tells stories the same way over and over.

Feeling that you must have every toy, every device, every piece of equipment merely places objects between you and your child. You have to work that much harder to provide them; work which robs your child of his most important stimulation — your company.

Those who become trapped in the cycle of getting and having spend their children's lives in a kind of fog. The best moments are lost forever.

Ask the question: Who really benefits from all this consumption?

54

INFLUENCE

Right mothering is honored from
generation to generation. Like an
old tree with untold roots, it holds
firm through countless storms.

Behave toward yourself with
loving kindness, and serenity
will emanate from you.

When you are serene,
your life is in order.

When your life is in order,
your family is harmonious.

Your family affects your
community. Your community
influences your culture.
Your culture influences the world.

How do I know?
Just by looking around.

55

ATTUNEMENT

The energy that comes from the
Infinite moves through you and
enlightens your being.

When you have released your fear
and found your Self, you can
be in harmony with your child
because you are attuned to
the same energy.

In this space you are relaxed and
soft, bendable. Things don't bother
you, energy flows. You can
walk the baby all night long;
her cries do not challenge you.

Your power is in place
without exerting it.

56

APPROVAL

A wise parent knows her
intuition is the only authority
worth listening to. She
understands its function and
filters advice through it.

Rigid styles characterize
the insecure parent who needs to
protect her own inner child with
fear. She is full of "don'ts."

A wise parent refrains from
too much talk. Her inner calm
brings peace to troubled hearts
and resolution to conflicts.
She doesn't need anyone's
approval but her own.

57

BE FIRM

At each stage of your child's life
she needs demonstrations of
your love and your support.

Your love comforts and accepts.
It is a mirror in which your child
sees herself as beautiful and
worthy.

Your support encourages and
affirms; it is a springboard
toward independence.

Too many rules turn facilitation into interference, affection into business. Let your child help set her own limits against which she can push now and then.

Be firm without being rigid. Your child will grow up with lots of healthy personal power.

58

Healthy Parenting

Healthy parenting can be a challenge if your own childhood wasn't healthy. It requires energy, attention, and constant restraint. These all come naturally from healthy parent-child bonds.

If the parenting you received was rigid, abandoning, or inconsistent, you may find yourself exhausted by your children. Realize that you need healing. Take time out to nurture yourself.

You can make the choice to be a
healthy parent. You can learn how
to trust what is happening and
behave appropriately. You can find
a healthy model and follow it.

Unhealthy parenting disables
with wounds that are hard to heal.
Right mothering is a potent
healer, readily available to the
natural wounds of life.

59

RESTRAINT

In bringing up children there is
nothing like restraint. This
requires deep roots in your own
spirituality, because it means
releasing your own ideas in favor
of perceiving each child's needs.

Prayer, meditation and the like
can help you stay centered
and aware of the deeper levels
of what is happening. Take the
time you need for your
spiritual growth.

Cultivate limitlessness,
and you will know how and
when to set limits for your
children.

60

MIRROR

As much as possible, let your
children find their own way.
Mother them delicately,
like frying eggplant.

Negative states will arise,
express, and pass away.
Allow this to happen. Help the
child to become aware of this
process gently, without intrusion.
The wise parent does not
fight fire with fire.

Be a mirror. Let your child see
how cause and effect works in life.
Too much interference and advice
gives power to opposing forces.

61

INDEPENDENCE

The mother's energy is so powerful because of her feminine receptivity. She yields and conquers through her calm.

The child's energy dominates. He feels so powerful! Only the mother knows it is her strength upon which he draws to build himself.

Thus both reach their goal of independence.

62

No blame

Knowing how things work
is helpful to you. But remember,
mothers have mothered since the
dawn of time, and it all seems to
work out in the end.

If you don't know your intuition,
it is no crime. However, if you
know how things work, you are
fortunate. Your behavior will be
more effective, your words will
have more power, your decisions
will be good ones.

Since ancient times people have revered those whose spiritual faculties are well developed.

63

ASSISTANCE

If you want to help your children
build themselves, you must act
without seeming to act. Through
gestures, small words, and
most of all through your own
example, your children will
gradually grow wings.

Your baby is learning to trust you.
Touch and hold her and smile
into her eyes. Allow her to feel
all her feelings.

Your toddler is learning to trust
the earth. Support and protect
him. Allow him to explore.

Your preschooler is learning to trust herself. Help her learn appropriate choices. Allow her to say no and test her limits.

Your young child is learning to trust relationships with others. Affirm his ability to learn how to express his feelings and ask for help. Allow him to ask questions.

Your older child is learning to trust society. Provide accurate information, offer problem-solving tools, and encourage responsibility. Allow her to

experience consequences while
remaining safe in your love
and support.

Your adolescent is learning to
trust himself as an adult.
Celebrate his growing up. Talk
about your own feelings at his
age. Allow him to explore choices
that may be different from yours.

Know your child's needs at each
stage and anticipate her struggles.
In this way you can offer assistance
without seeming to assist.

64

> # NOW

Love your children while they
are small. Spend time with them
now. Don't put it off for a
single moment.

The rigid tree begins as a pliant
sapling. A huge building begins
as a shovelful of dirt. A thousand-
mile journey begins under
your feet.

Everything depends on early
influences. You can't go back later
and bond with your children in
the same way.

Many parents get anxious with their teenagers and try to make up for lost time. When the child needs wings, they try to root him and spoil everything.

Conscious mothering requires careful choices, from beginning to end.

65

EXPERTS

The ancient mothers knew. There
was no need for books and experts.

Today we have lost much.
We need to relearn the Way.

Be cautious about what the experts
tell you. What sounds complex
and clever may have no roots.
Wisdom has no cleverness in it.
It is pure and simple, and when it is
practiced the results are obvious.

The wise assist a child's being
rather than his doing.

66

EQUANIMITY

The sea is the greatest of all the waters because it allows the rivers and streams to empty into it.

Parents with the greatest power in their children's lives are those to which the child can go without fear.

The wise mother facilitates her child's growth with firm, loving kindness. She receives his mistakes and tantrums with equanimity.

Because she does not push, harass, or manipulate, she does not invite rebellion. Her children love and respect her and trust her with their pain.

67

YOUR TREASURES

Everyone says the Eternal One
is great. Because it is great it is
beyond our comprehension.
If we could hold it in our minds,
it would be limited. If it is limited,
it is not the Way.

There are three treasures which
are invaluable to you as a parent:

The first is kindness. The second is
simplicity. The third is humility.

If you are kind, you can act with
courage to support and protect
your children.

If you keep your life simple, you have lots of time to give them.

If you know yourself as a human being — no more, no less — you teach your children without imposing on them.

A parent who is protective without being kind, whose life is busy and complicated, who demands respect and expects perfection, loses her children in the end.

Loving kindness, simplicity, and humility are the treasures your children will inherit.

EMPOWERMENT

A good soldier is never hateful.
A good fighter is not angry.
A good employer encourages
leadership.

The best parenting shows
choices rather than
delivering ultimatums.

Empowerment is the natural
means to grow a good
human being.

BATTLES

When your children push against their limits and your boundaries, consider the advice of the ancient strategists: do not allow yourself to be baited into fighting fire with fire. Keep your center. Calmly and clearly show them their choices.

This is winning the battle without showing your sword.

If you try to overpower your
children you will discover a simple
truth: their power is greater
than yours! Thus you surrender
your treasure and respect is lost.

In a battle of wills, loving kindness
is the only weapon that conquers.

70

A ROAD
LESS TRAVELED

Bringing up children in this way
is easy to understand and easy to
do. But not many parents are able
to follow it.

The Way is ancient and follows
truth. It is known to those who
are truly human. But parents
today have lost their roots
and rely on the latest gimmicks
and the opinions of medical
technicians.

The wise are known only by
a few. Their wisdom is concealed.
The wise mother's precious gem
is hidden in the pocket of
her apron.

DON'T KNOW

Admit you don't know
everything. Admit you may
not know anything.

To pretend that you know
when you don't leads to pain.
When you are tired of pain,
you will no longer create it.
This is the secret of good health.

WONDER

Children who grow up with no
spirituality — with no sense of
wonder — will struggle with
depression as adults.

Do not impose rational thinking
on your children too early.
Do not oppress them with
adult reality.

Because you don't pressure
them to grow up, they can
grow naturally and keep their
sweetness.

The wise parent can be childlike
but is not irresponsible,
loves herself but is not selfish.
She is spiritual but not dogmatic.

73

COURAGE

There are two kinds of courage.

There is the passionate bravery
which gets people killed.
This kind of courage is inherent;
either you have it or you don't.
It is the bravery of a mother
who would die shielding her child
from a killer's bullet.

The second type of courage is
developed through daily practice.
It is the inner strength to do what
must be done, to make rational
plans and carry them out, to face
difficulty and overcome obstacles.

It is the bravery of a mother
who makes personal sacrifices
for her children's well-being,
and then is able to let them go
to their own destinies.

74

PUNISHMENT

Many parents discover too late
that one cannot raise children well
with punishment as the core of
discipline. Hit your child and
eventually the child's rage will be
greater than your censure.

Prisons are filled with "well-
disciplined" people.

A good parent helps a child
to learn how his behavior affects
his own life through natural
consequences. This is how true
inner discipline is cultivated.

A master carpenter cuts cleanly and quickly and makes furniture which endures. When you deliver harsh, judgmental consequences, you are trying to do nature's job. Like an inexperienced carpenter, you are bound to make a mess of it and only hurt yourself.

• ⌣

75

CRITICISM

Children starve if their parents
eat all the food.

Children rebel if their parents
brook no compromise.

Children have no love for life if
their parents squeeze it out of
them. They spend their lives
grieving for their lost joy.

Begin to notice when you are
critical and controlling with your
child. Observe yourself and check
your behavior before it gets
acted out.

Find out what you need and
give it to yourself. When the little
child in you gets the love, support,
and encouragement it needs,
your critical behavior will
naturally disappear.

FLEXIBILITY

Human bodies are gentle and flexible when living but hard and stiff when dead.

Living plants are tender and green when living but dry and brittle when dead.

To be hard and unbending is to be dead. Without flexibility, there is no juice. What is the point of living then?

BALANCE

When people are in harmony
with spiritual laws, everything is
in balance. The excess is reduced,
the deficient is expanded,
everyone's needs are met and
life is full of joy.

When we lose the Way, we lose
our balance and life is full of pain.
We take from those who do not
have enough and give to those
who have too much.

A mother who walks in balance
has more than enough. She enters
her children's lives and surrounds
them with love when their heart-
reserves are low. She allows them
to do the same for her.

She understands the cyclic nature
of things, the way the bow
contracts and expands to receive
and release the arrow.

78

PARADOX

There is nothing more receptive
and flowing than water,
yet there is nothing better for
polishing stone.

A mother's nature is paradox.
Your strength is in gentleness.
Your authority is in receptivity.
Your power is in letting go.

RESOLUTION

As your children grow up,
there is bound to be some
unresolved pain. There was the
time you couldn't make it to the
third grade play. The time you
struck your child in anger. The
painful divorce which could not
be adequately explained.

A wise parent recognizes her
failings and accepts what is.
There is room in life for remorse,
and for forgiveness. There is
room in our hearts for ourselves,
and for one another.

SIMPLICITY

Keep your life simple and
serenity will follow.

Like a small country with little
need for supersonic travel,
a simple life has little need for
tension and stress.

Give your children yourself and
the need for things is minimal.

HONESTY

Tell the truth.

Say what is happening.

Allow what is, and allow it to be known.

Bring your children up in a home which is clean and clear and honest. There is no greater legacy you can give them.

About the Author

Vimala McClure lives and writes in Boulder, Colorado. She is the author of the classic *Infant Massage: A Handbook for Loving Parents* and founder of the International Association of Infant Massage Instructors. She has been practicing and teaching Tantra yoga since 1971.

She has also written *A Woman's Guide to Tantra Yoga, The Ethics of Love: Using Yoga's Timeless Wisdom to Heal Yourself, Your Family & the Earth,* and a book for children: *Bangladesh: Rivers in a Crowded Land.*

As well as being a writer, Vimala is a textile artist. Her quilts have won awards in regional and national shows, have been featured in national magazines, and are exhibited in galleries and private collections.

Vimala has three teenage children.

BIBLIOGRAPHY

English, Jane and Gia-Fu Feng, translators. Lao Tsu. *Tao Te Ching*. New York: Vintage Books, 1972.

Heider, John. *The Tao of Leadership*. Atlanta: Humanics New Age, 1985.

Iyer, Raghavan, Ed. Lao Tzu. *Tao Te Ching: The Book of Perfectibility*. London: Concord Grove Press, 1983.

Lau, D. C., translator. Lao Tzu. *Tao Te Ching*. London: Penguin Books, 1963.

Waley, Arthur. *The Way and Its Power*. New York: Grove Press, 1958.

Wu, John C.H., translator. Lao Tzu. *Tao Teh Ching*. Boston: Shambhala, 1989.

Enjoy these other inspiring works by Vimala McClure:

INFANT MASSAGE
A Handbook for Loving Parents

Start your baby's life out right with healthy, joyous intimacy. A massage is more than relaxation for an infant; it is an unparalleled communication of love, security, and acceptance. It also has the benefit of resolving colic, gassiness, and other common troubles of infancy. Fully illustrated with photographs that take you step by step through the massage.

"*Infant Massage* is recommended to our more than 100,000 members, with its beautiful photographs illustrating the touching and holding of an infant as important considerations for good mothering."

— *Viola Lennon*, Board of Directors,
La Leche League International

A WOMAN'S GUIDE TO TANTRA YOGA

A gentle introduction for women to a path in which all life is spiritualized. Included are chapters on yoga practices and the philosophy on which they are based. The author simply and clearly explains the universal outlook of Tantra Yoga, and shows the relationship between body, mind, and spirit. Covered are topics such as kundalini, the cakras, yoga's creation theory, karma, psychic development, yoga postures, beauty secrets of the yogis, meditation, mental outlook, ethics, and family life. Beautifully illustrated with a complete set of exercises.

"McClure is a trustworthy guide, a spiritual friend whose advice is as calm and as sensible as our own real hearts and minds."

— *The Bookreader*